"Flash" The Traffic Camera

Written By: C Dudley-Dance

Illustrations By: Amanda J. Coar

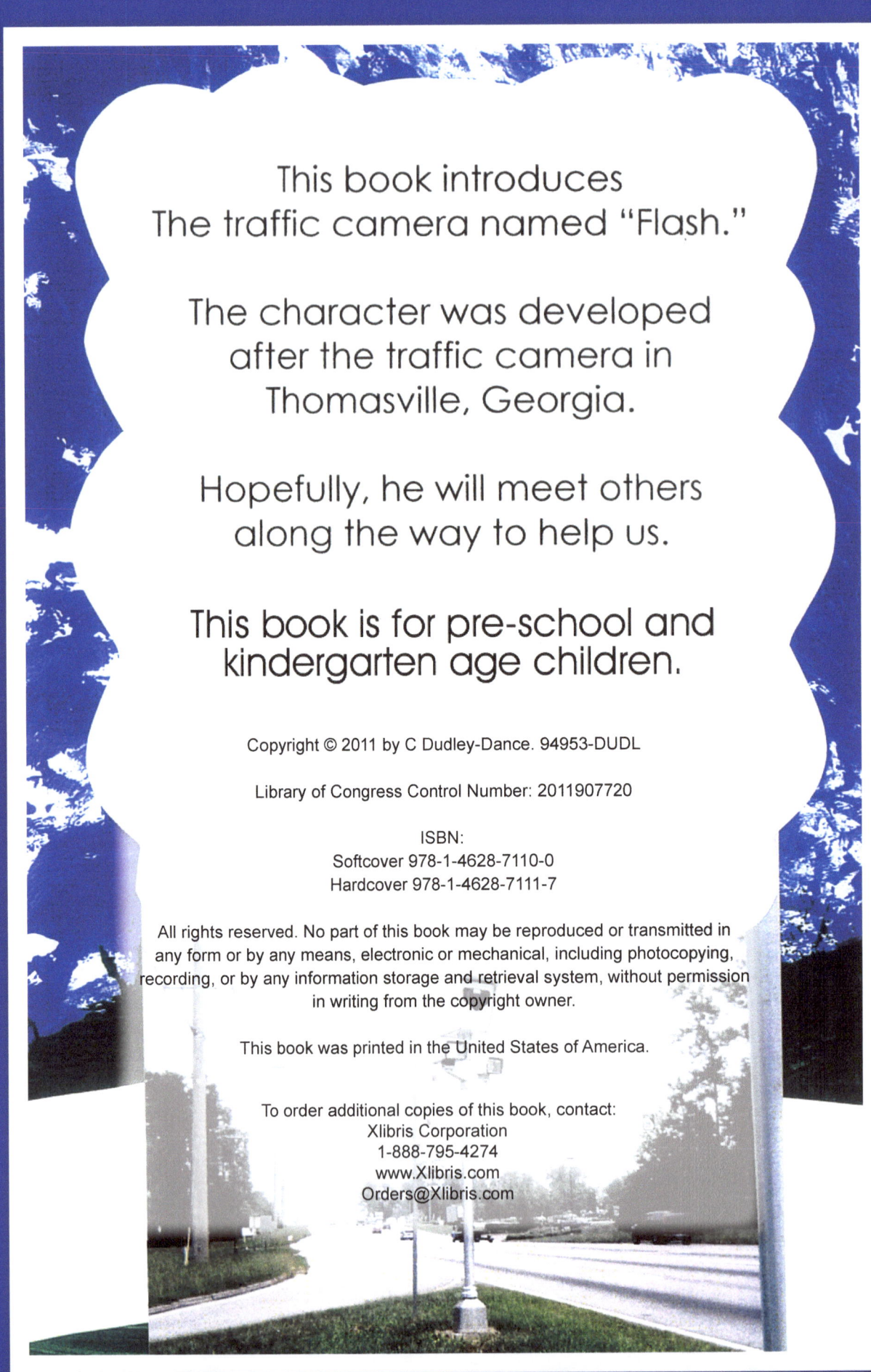

This book introduces
The traffic camera named "Flash."

The character was developed
after the traffic camera in
Thomasville, Georgia.

Hopefully, he will meet others
along the way to help us.

This book is for pre-school and
kindergarten age children.

To order additional copies of this book, contact:
Xlibris Corporation
1-888-795-4274
www.Xlibris.com
Orders@Xlibris.com

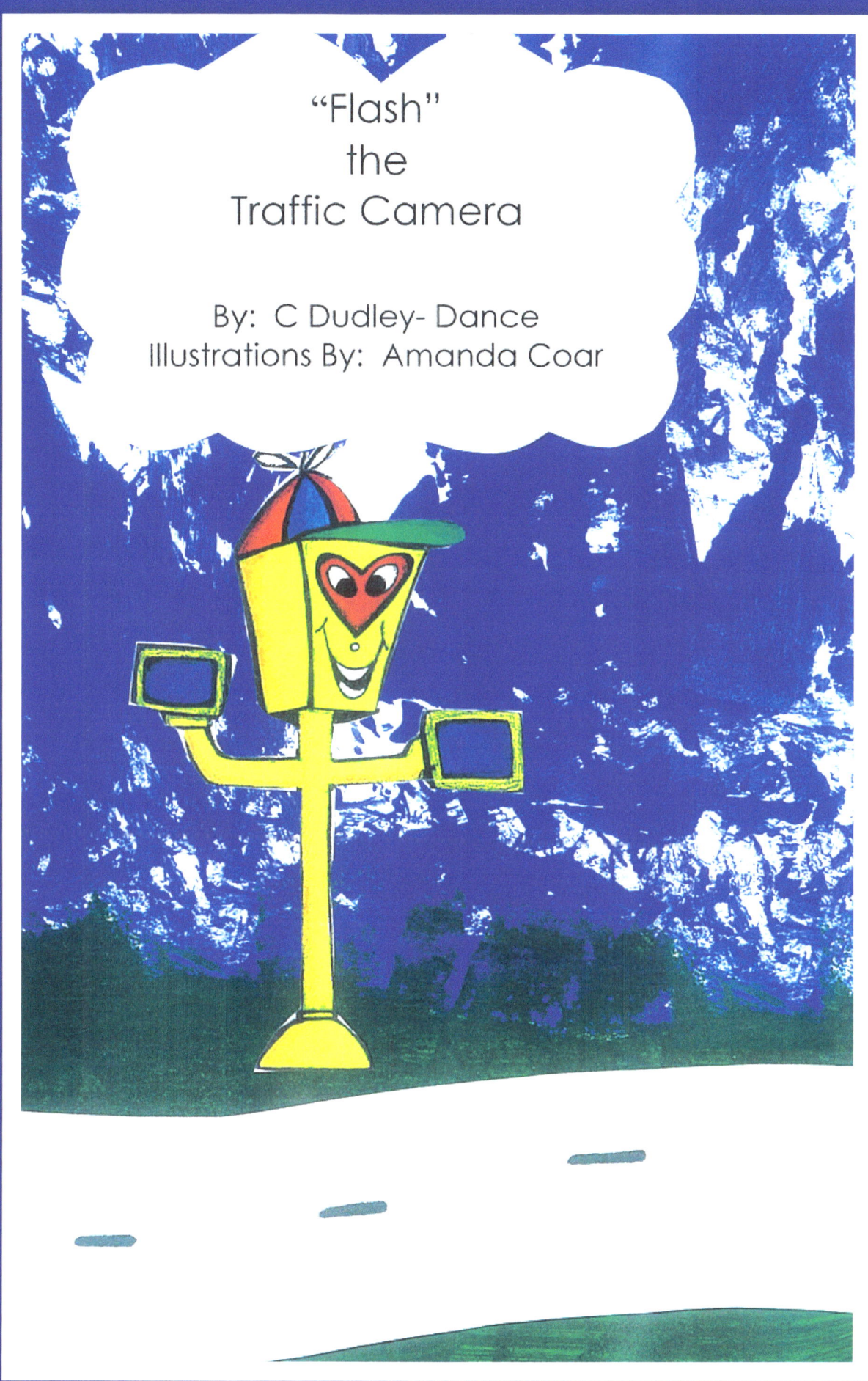

"Flash"
the
Traffic Camera

By: C Dudley- Dance
Illustrations By: Amanda Coar

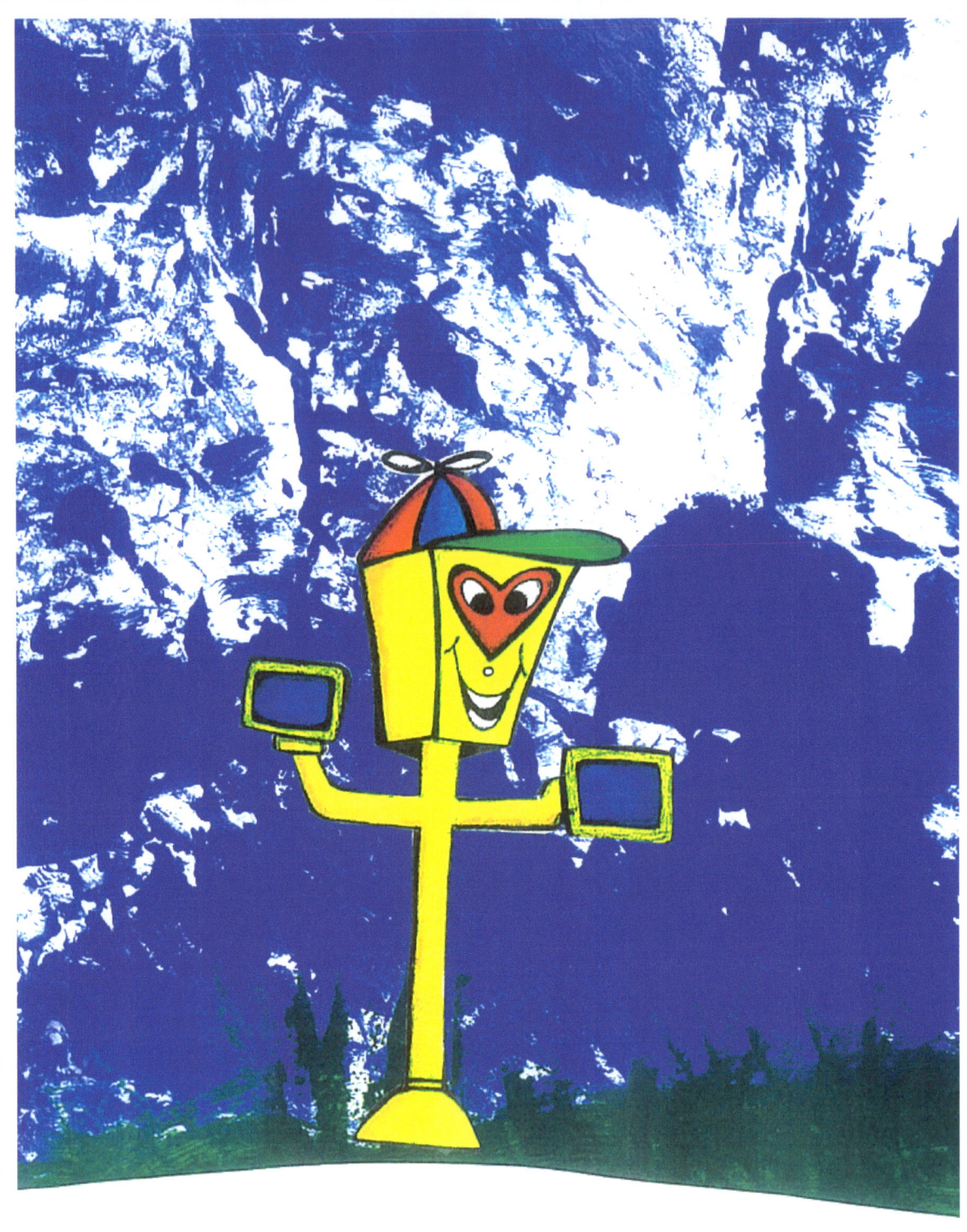

His blue hands flash for us to see....

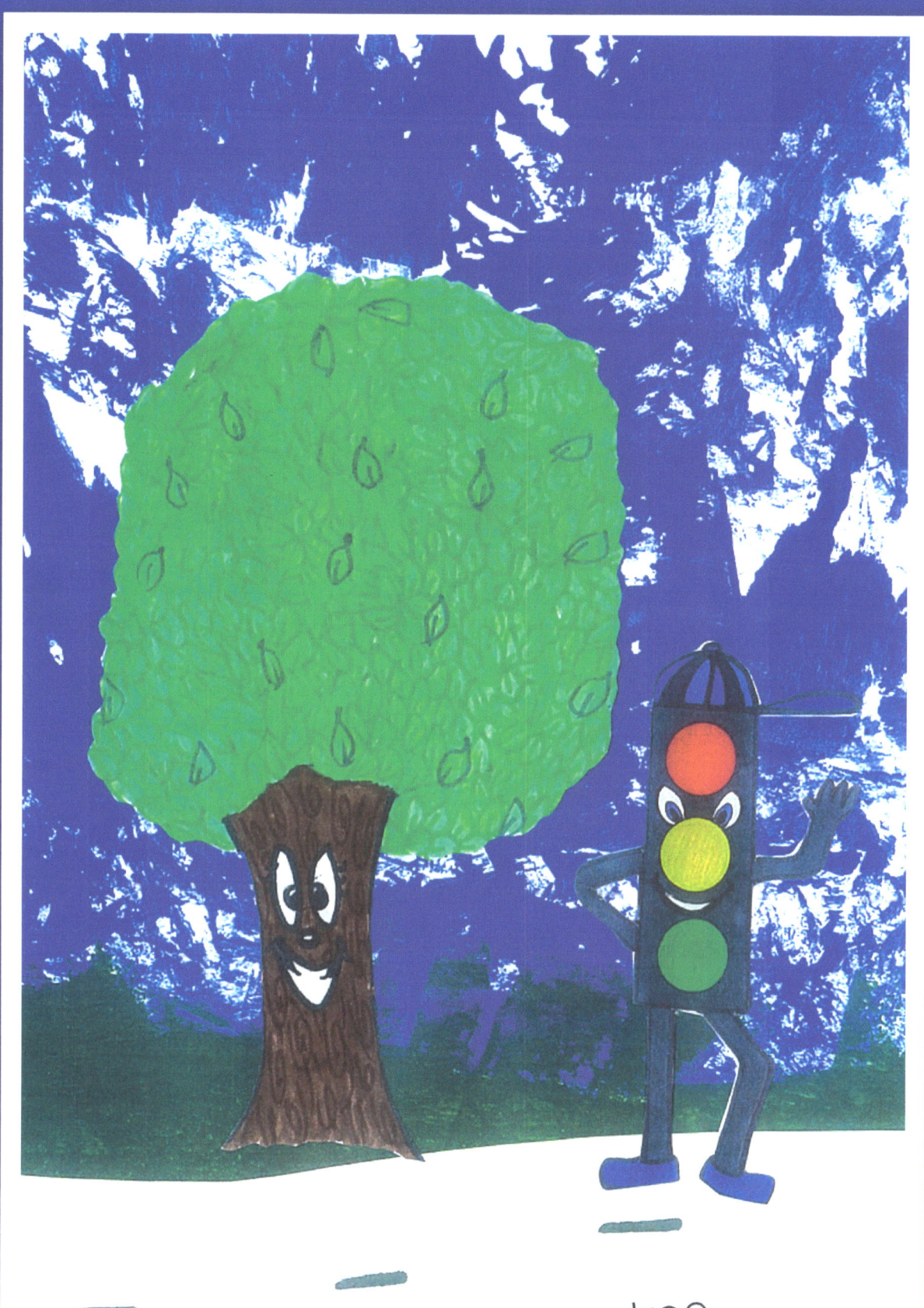

the traffic light near a tree.

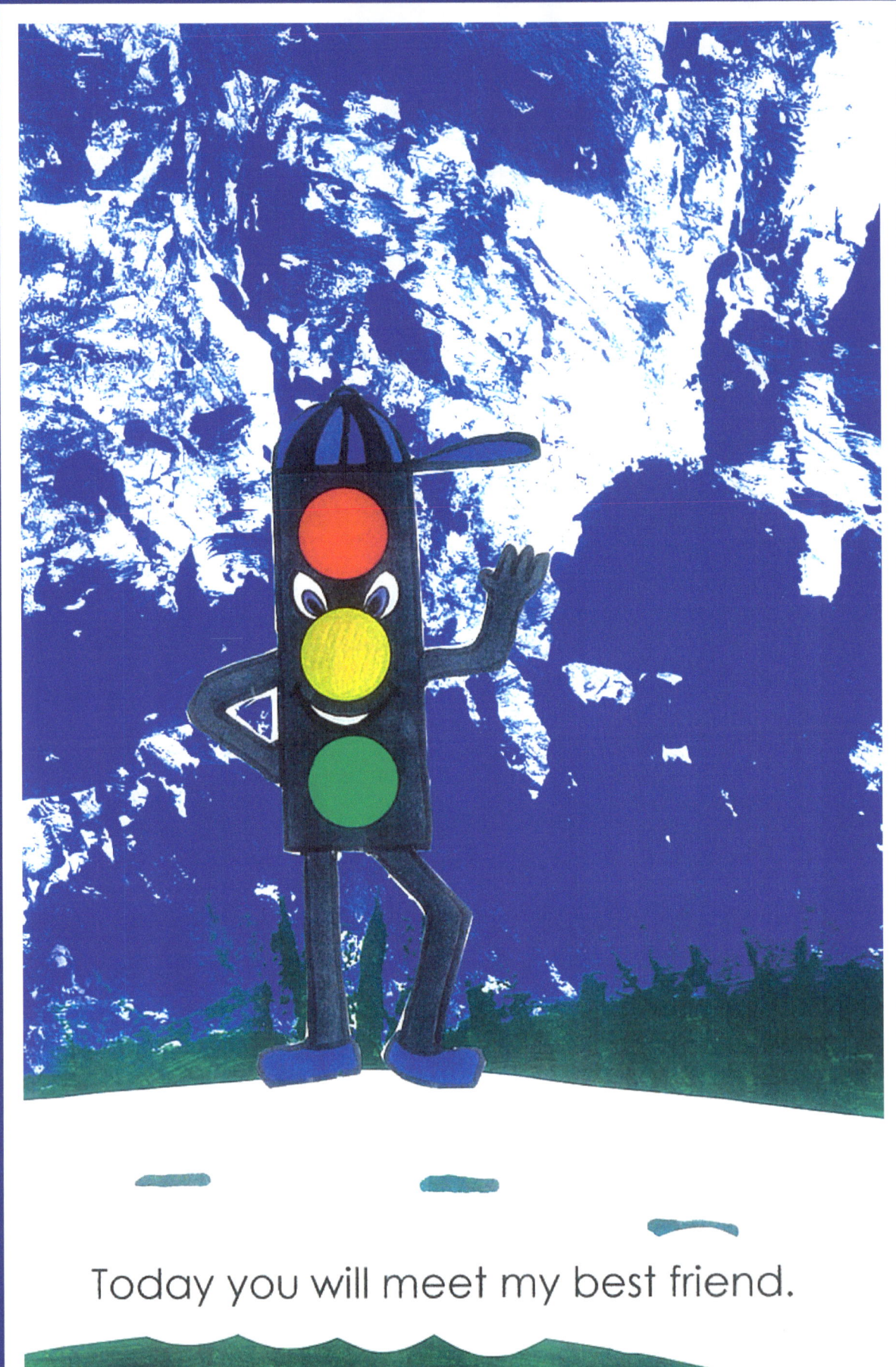

Today you will meet my best friend.

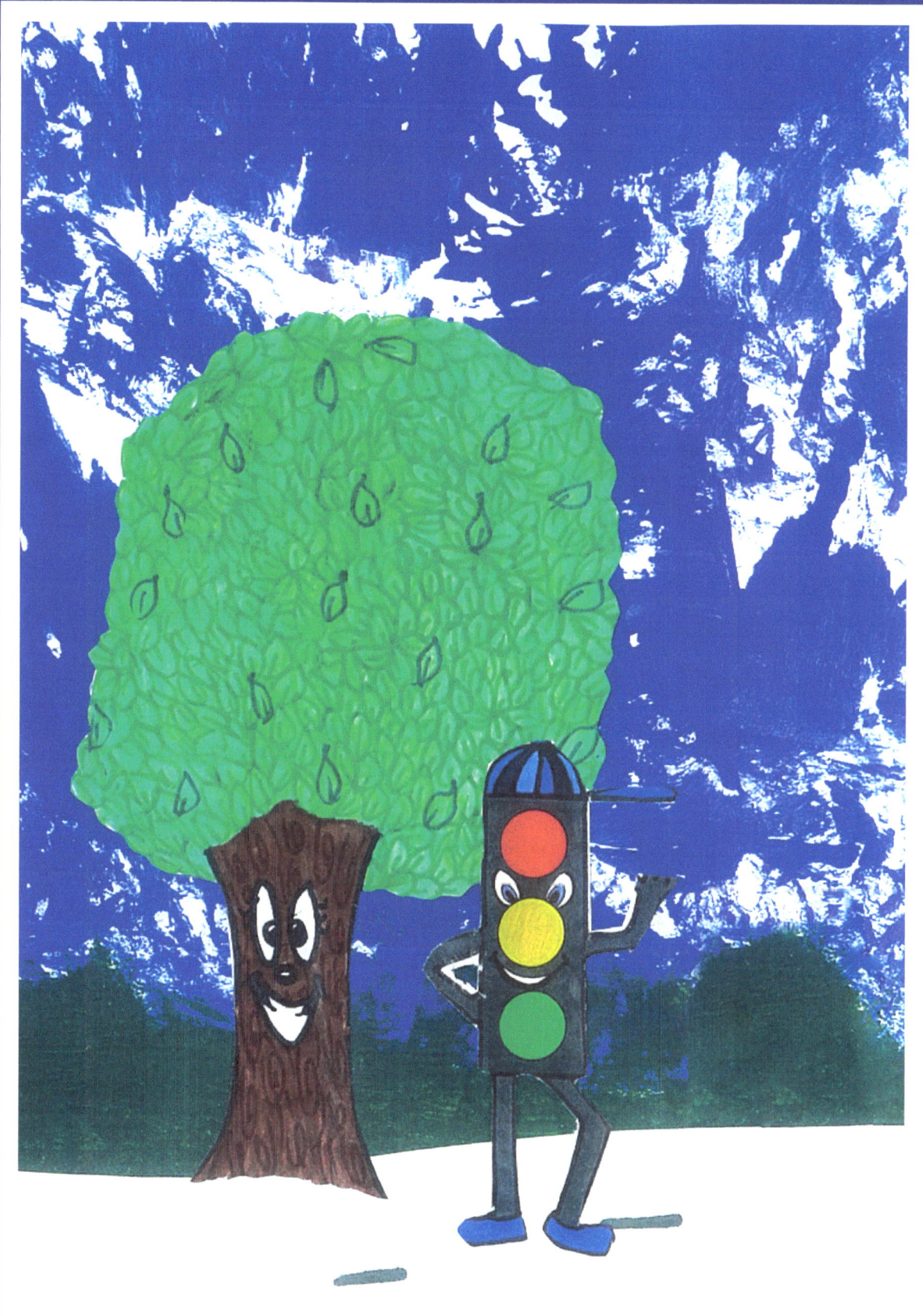

"Tom the Light" is around the bend.

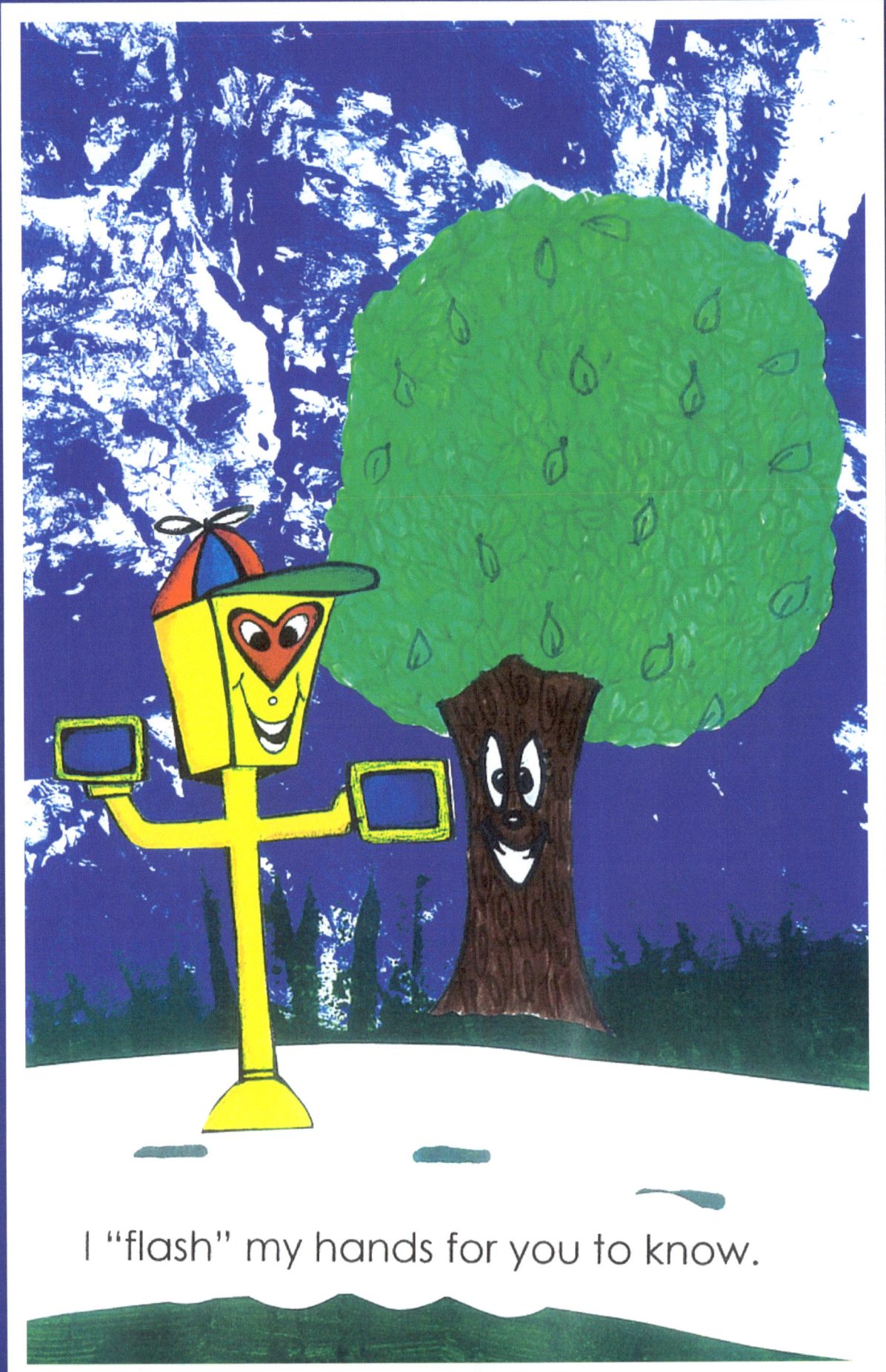

I "flash" my hands for you to know.

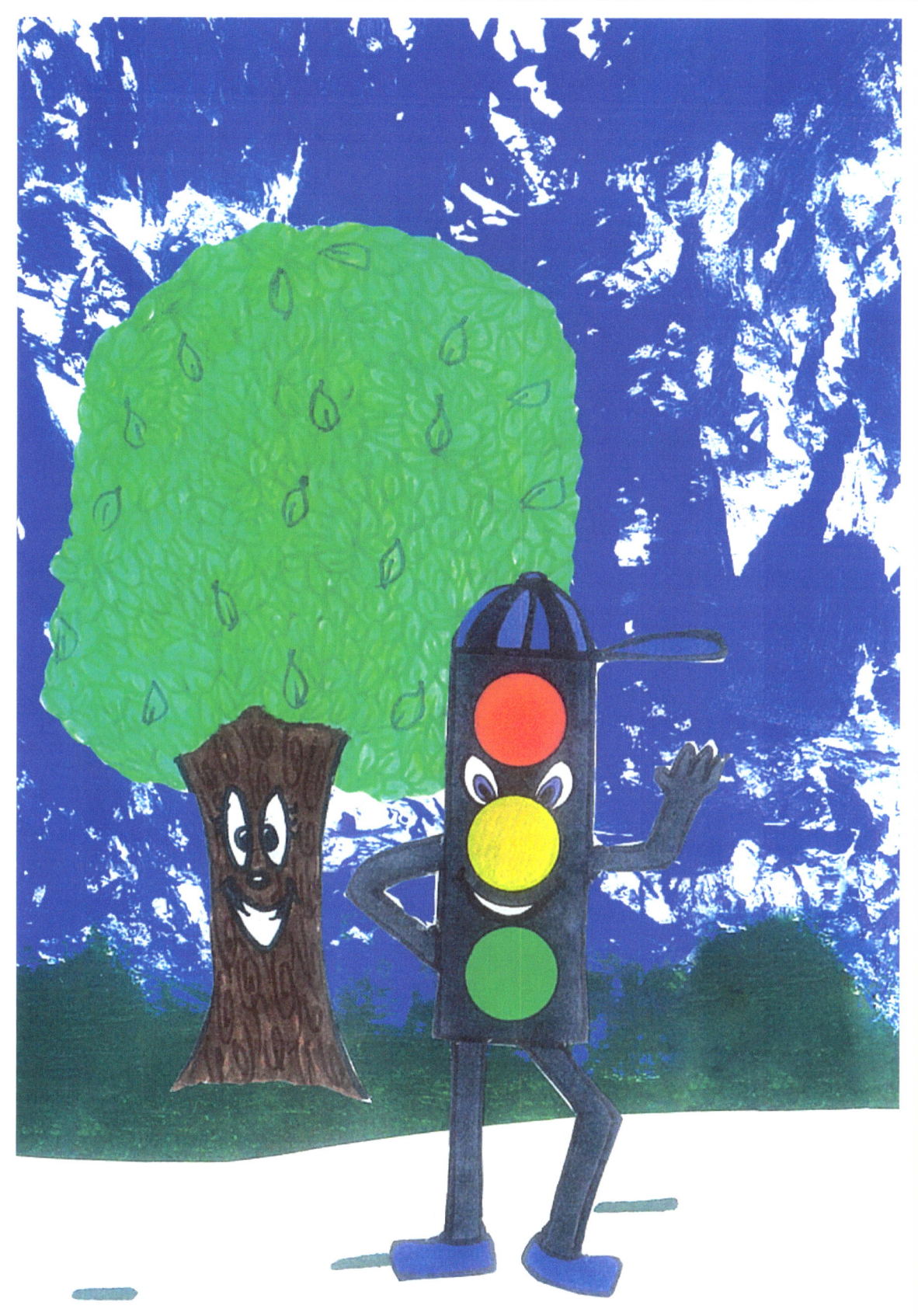

Ahead is a traffic light, please start to slow

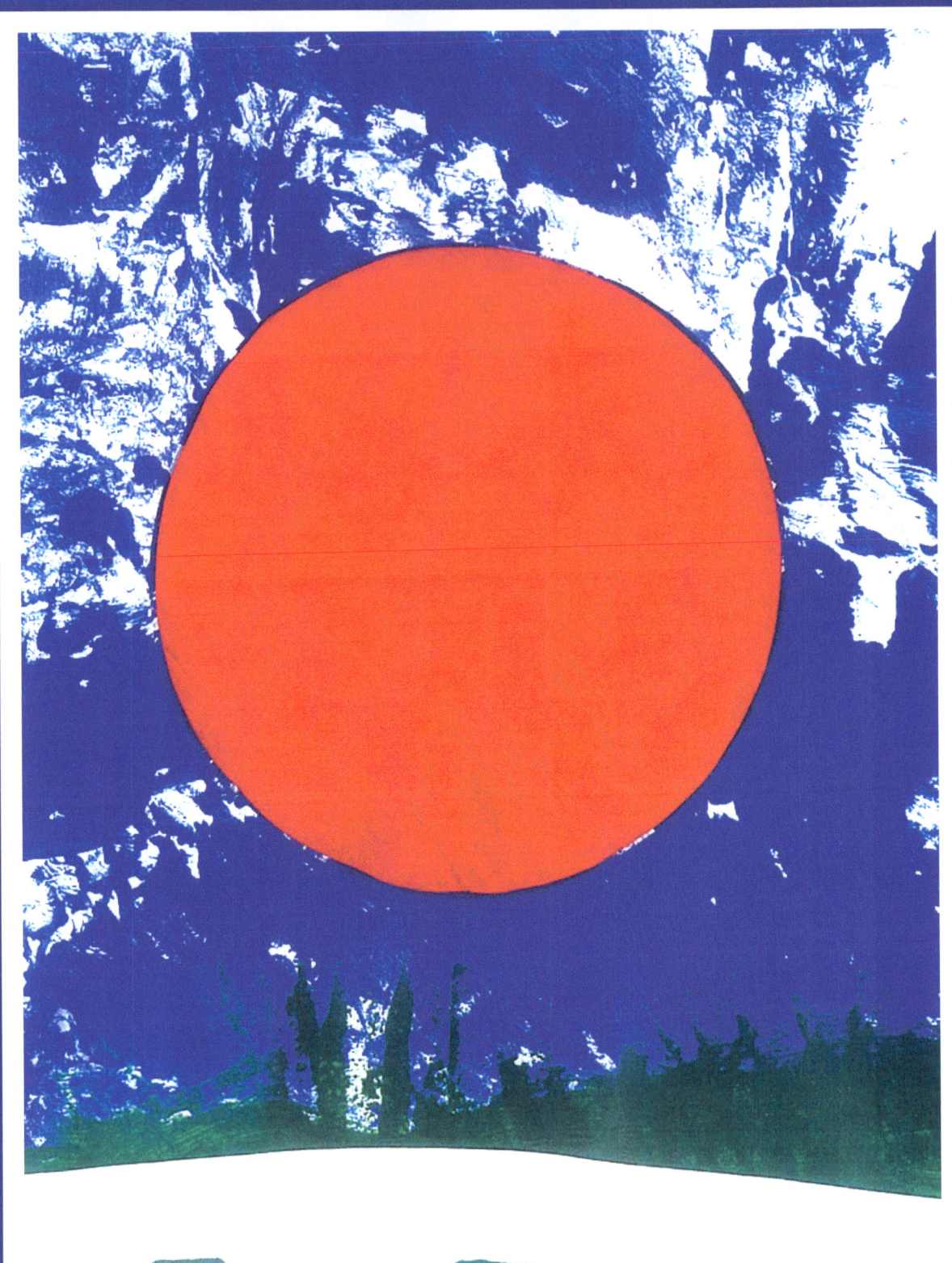

Remember: Red says "Stop."

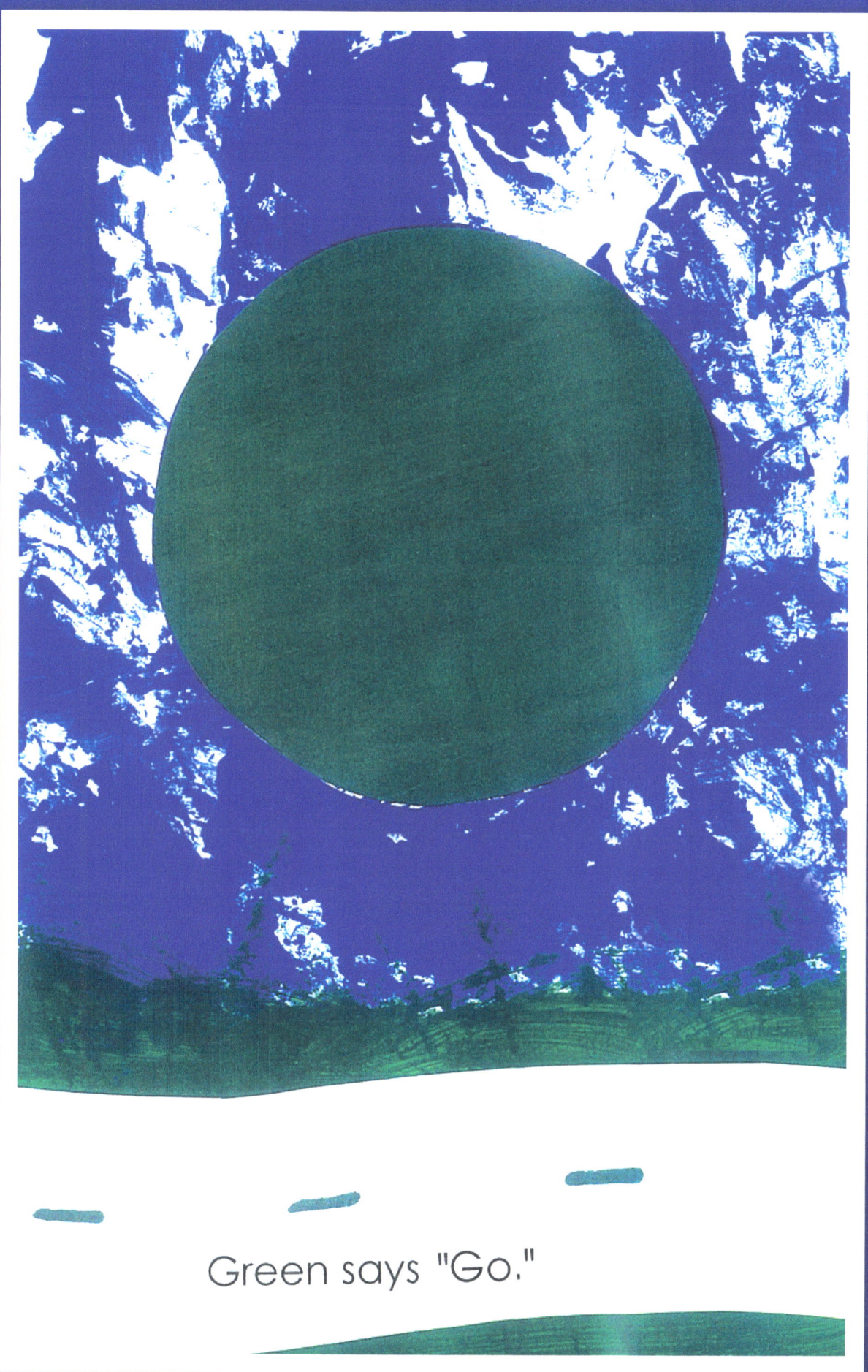

Green says "Go."

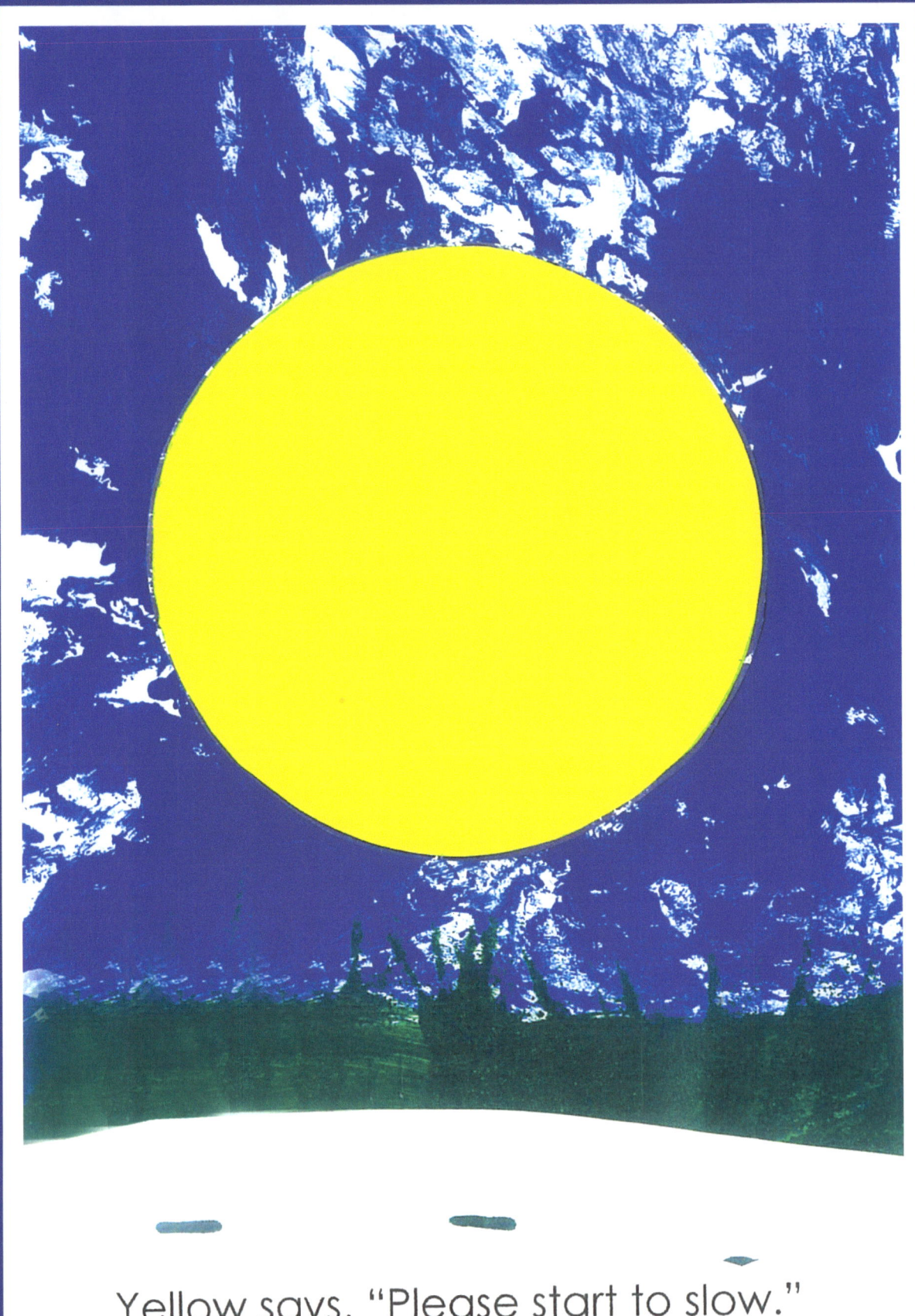

Yellow says, "Please start to slow."

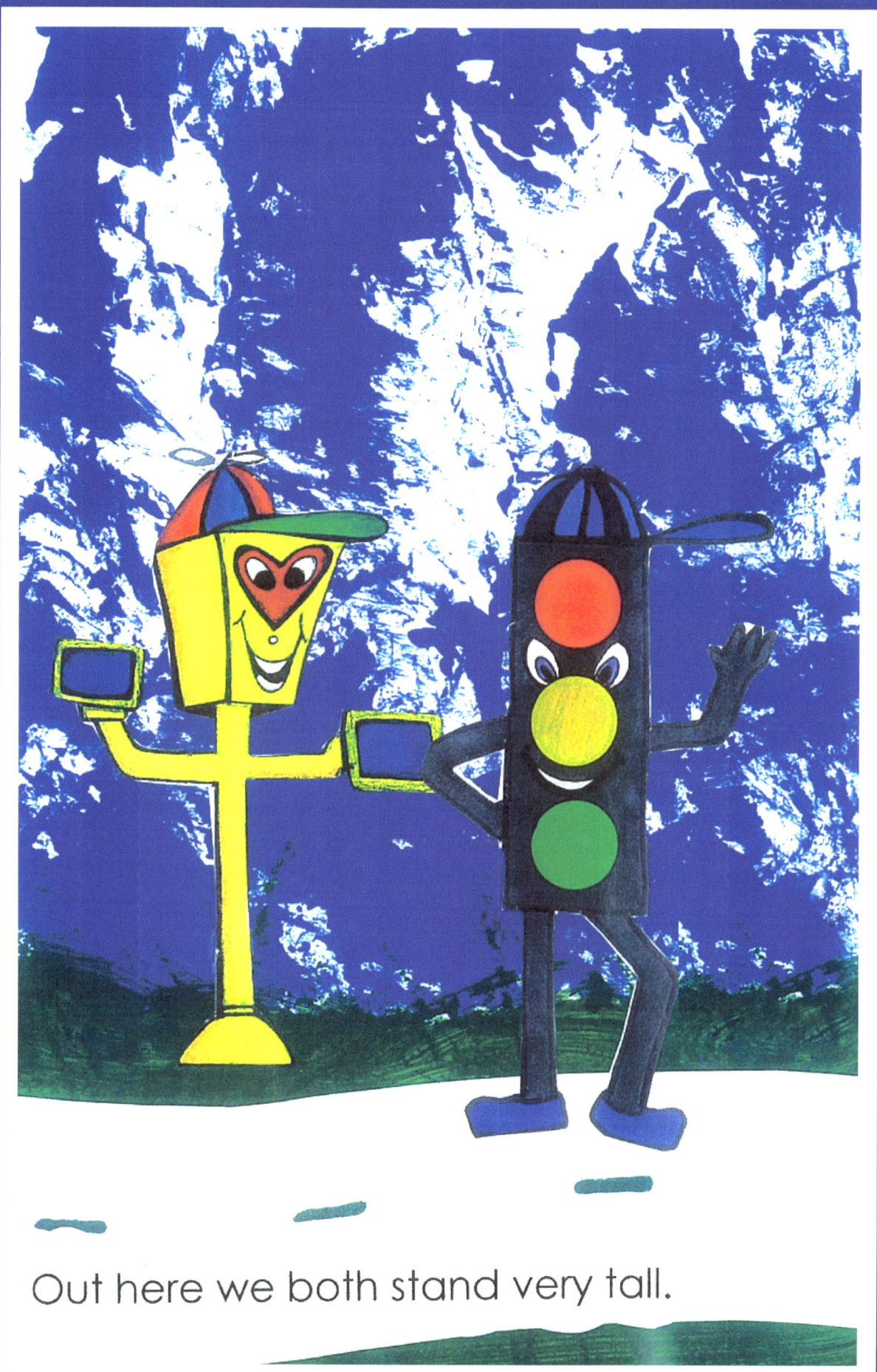

Out here we both stand very tall.

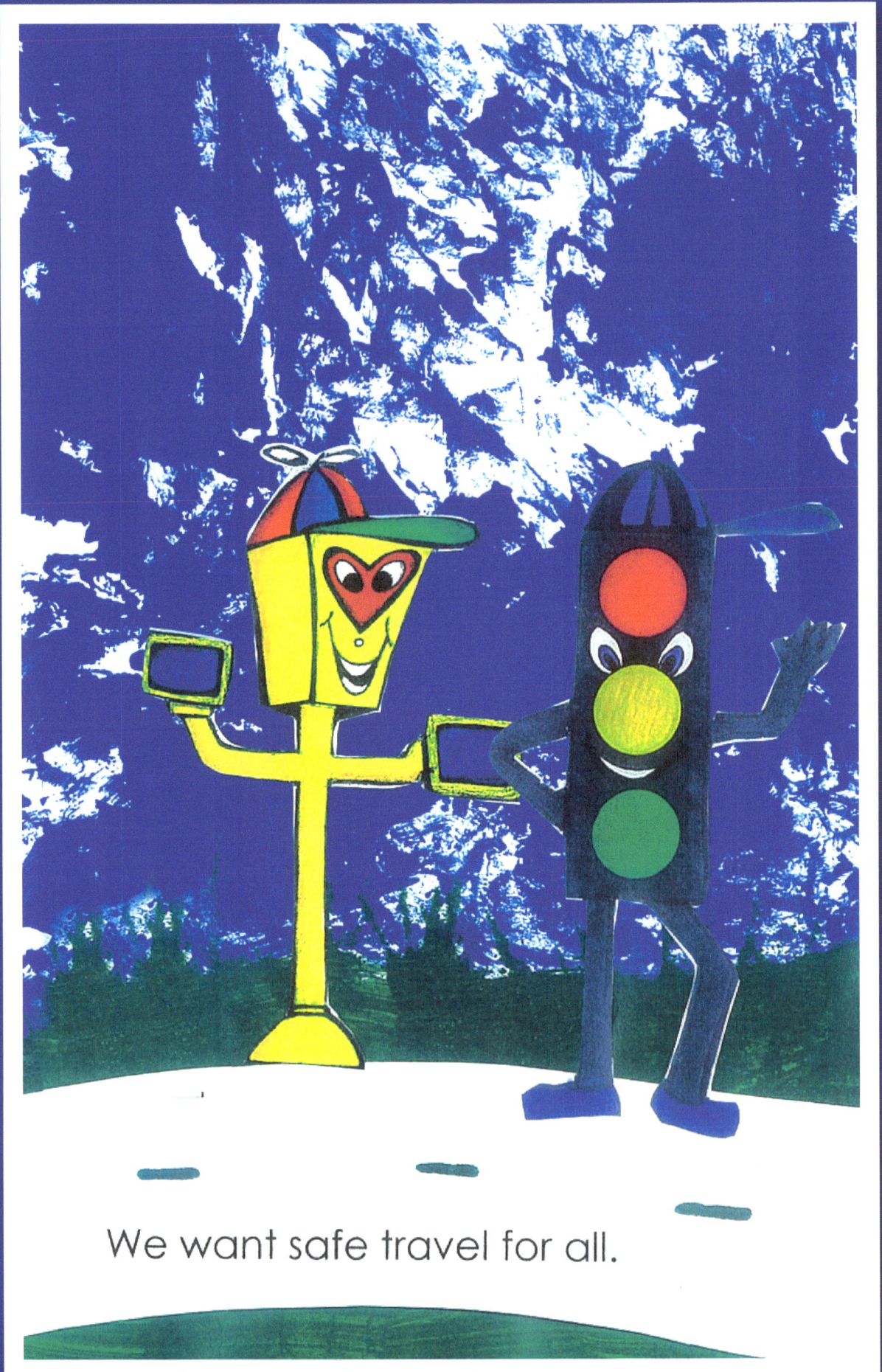

We want safe travel for all.

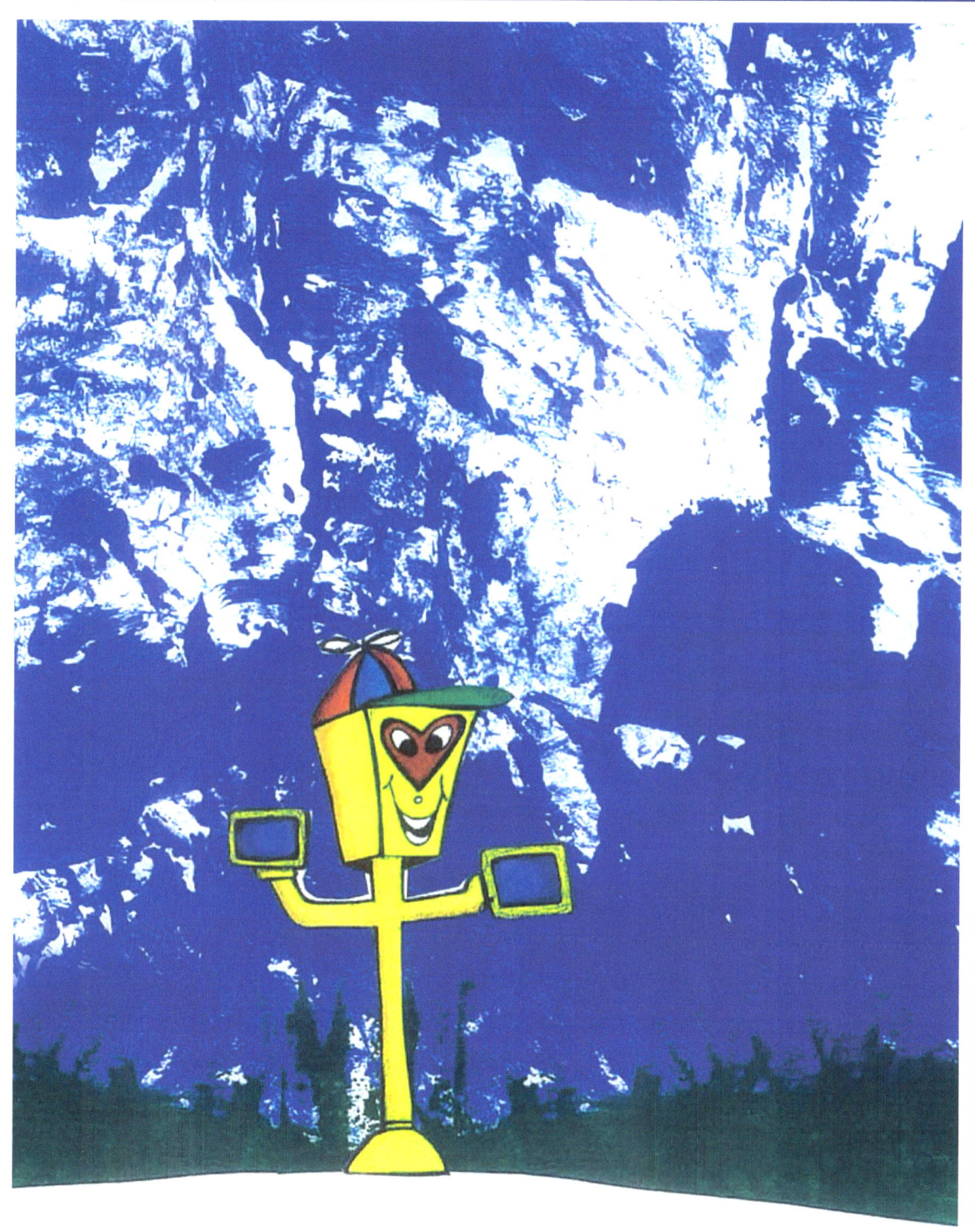

Tom and I are standing here.

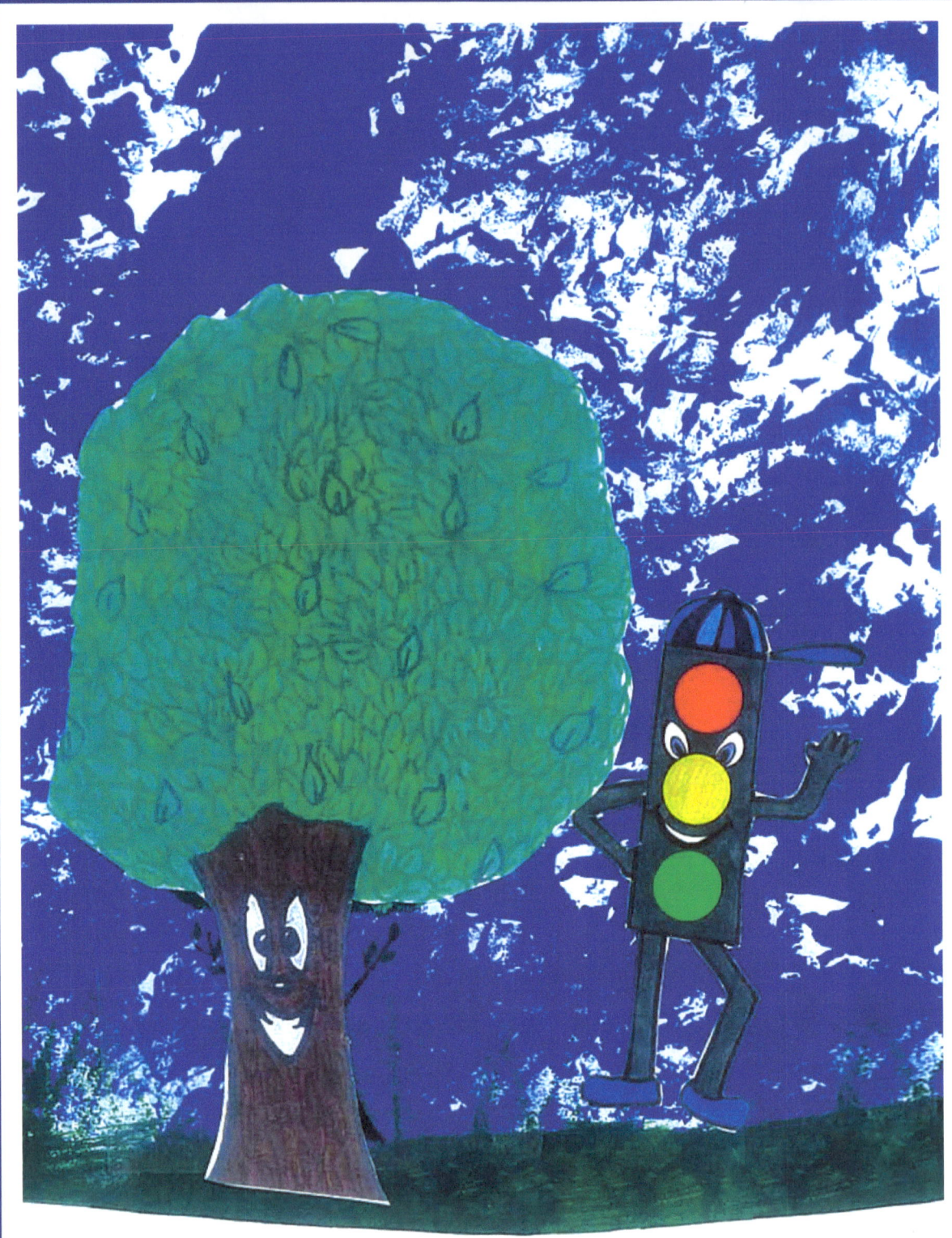

We know that Sammy the School Bus
is very near.

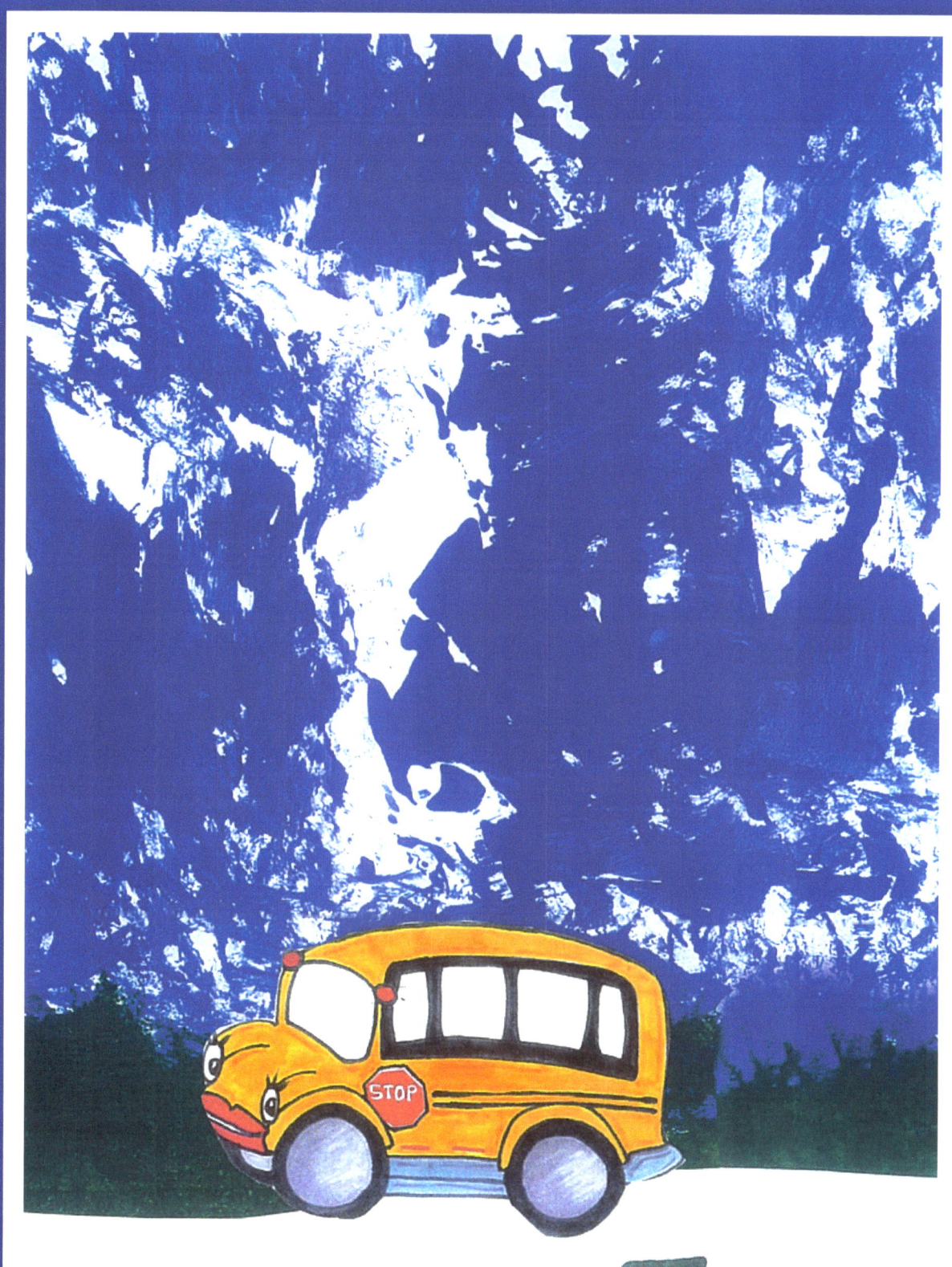

Meet Sammy, the School Bus, our friend.

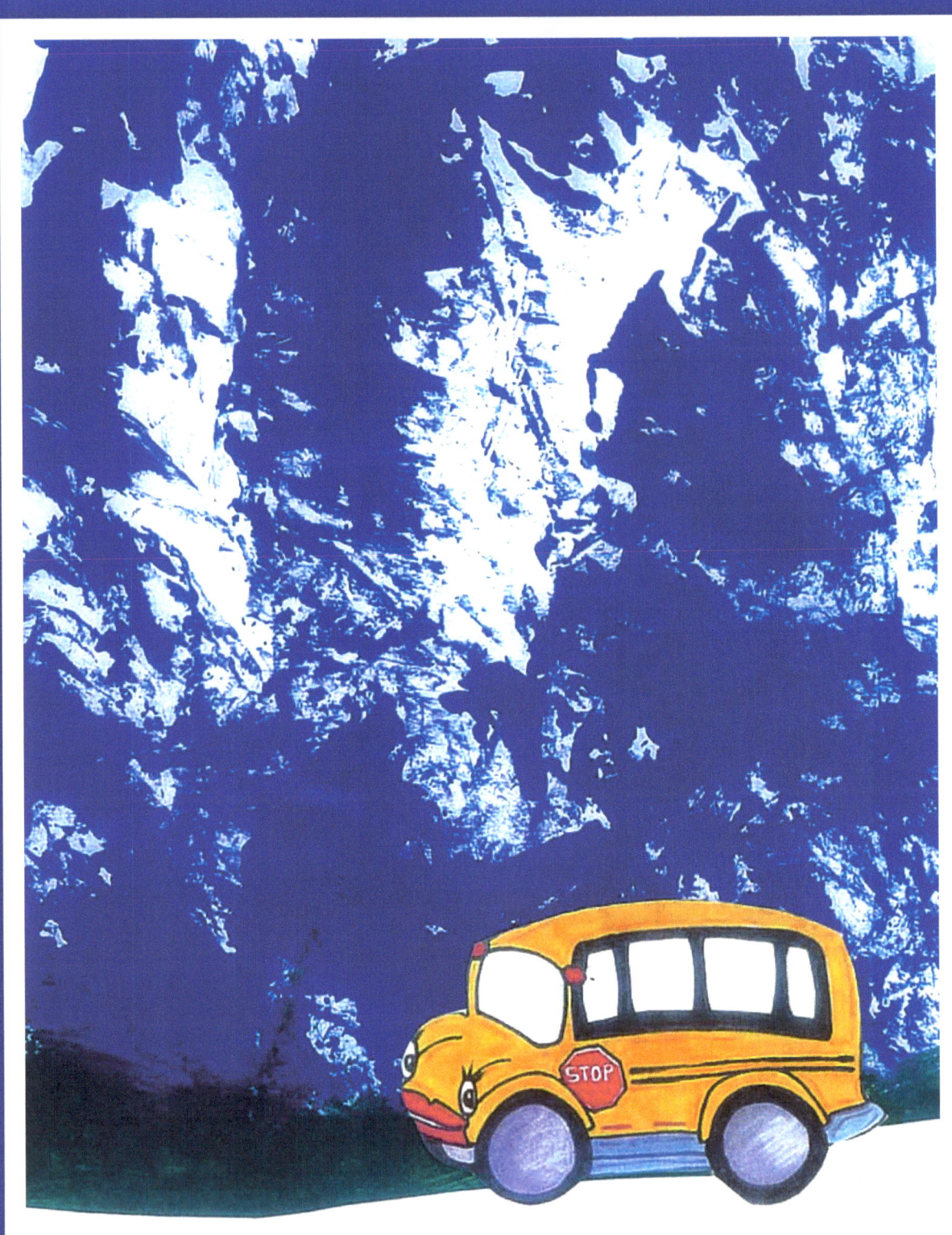

He is coming around the bend.

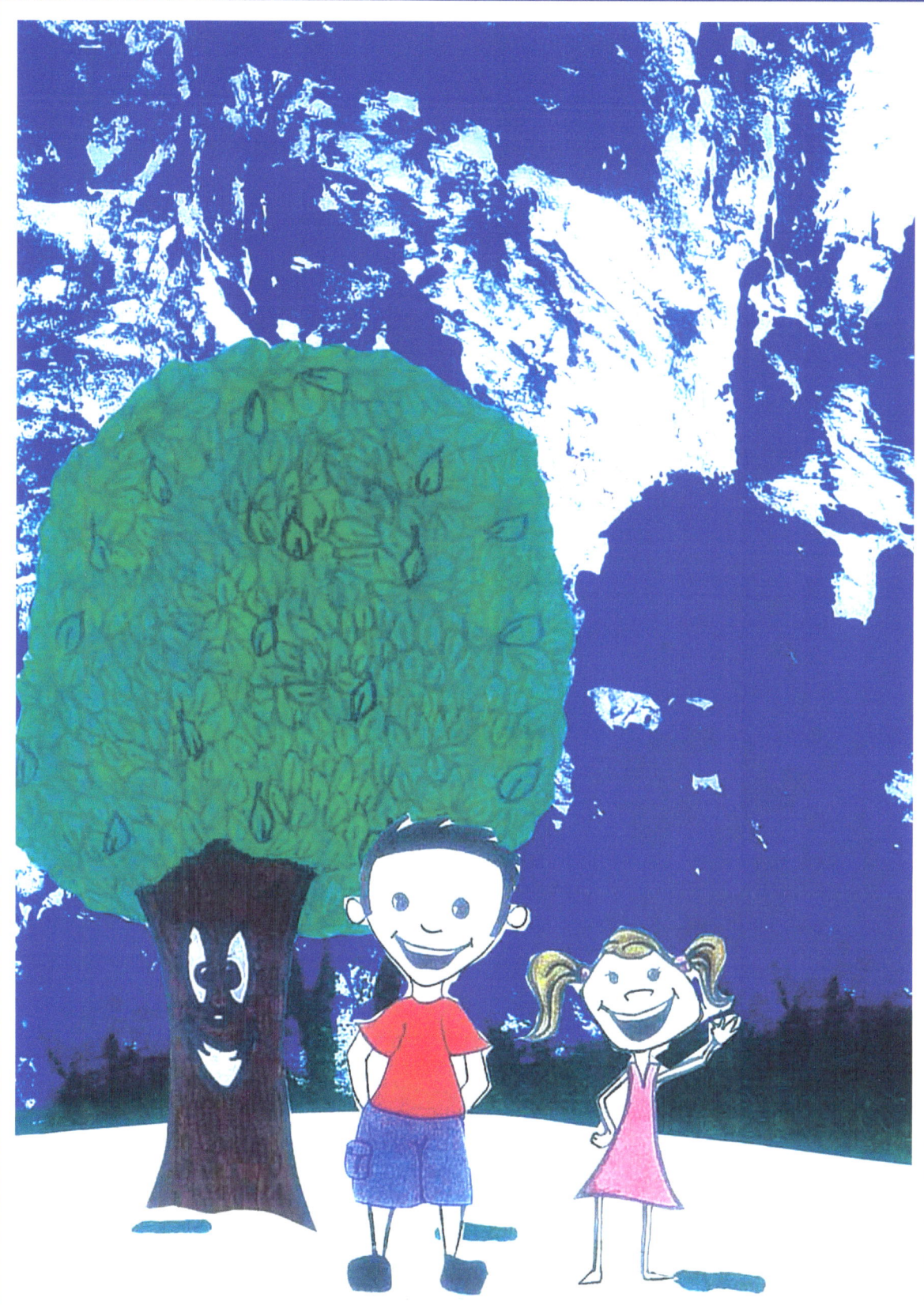

Sammy takes children safely to school.

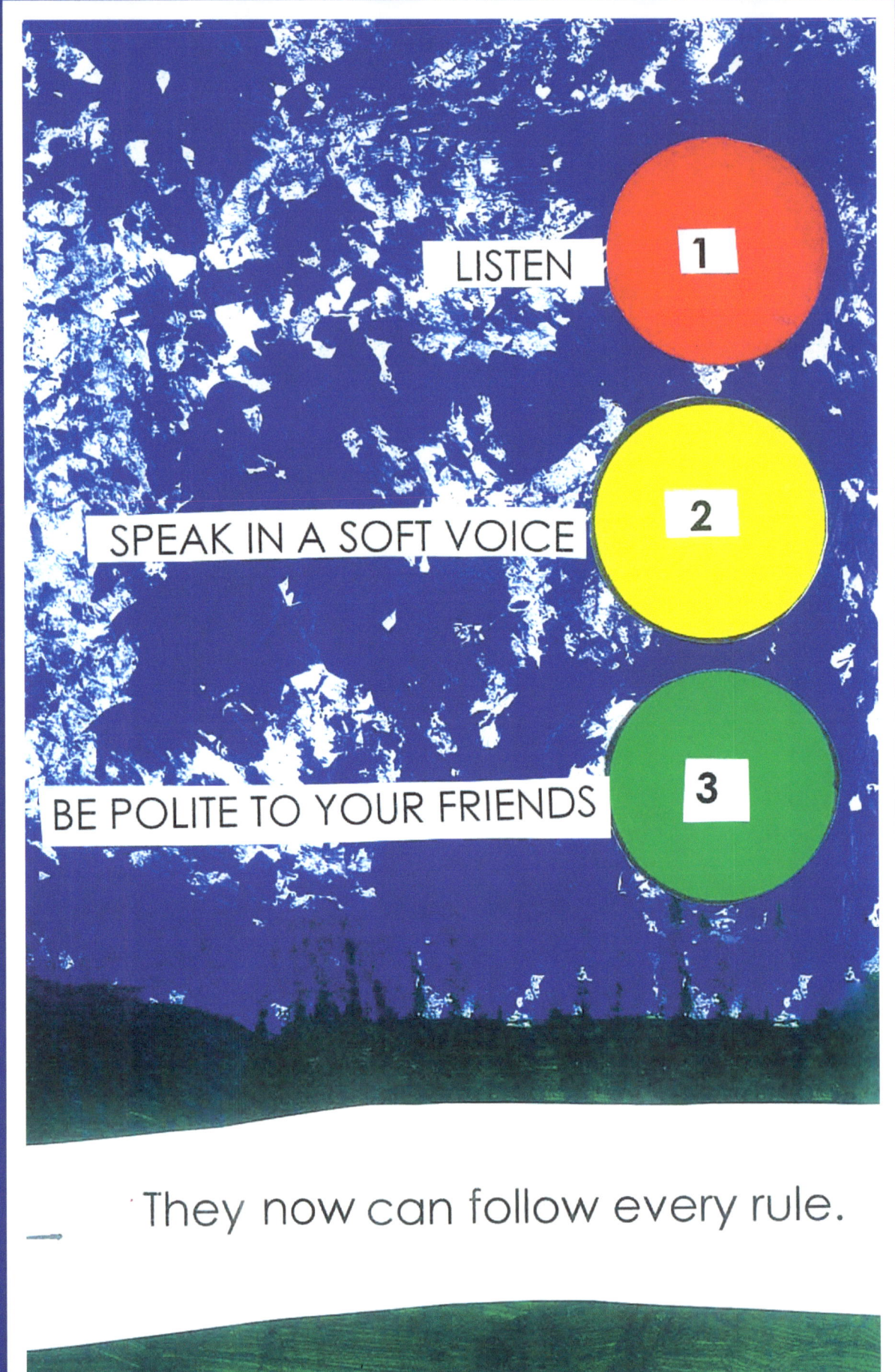

LISTEN 1

SPEAK IN A SOFT VOICE 2

BE POLITE TO YOUR FRIENDS 3

They now can follow every rule.

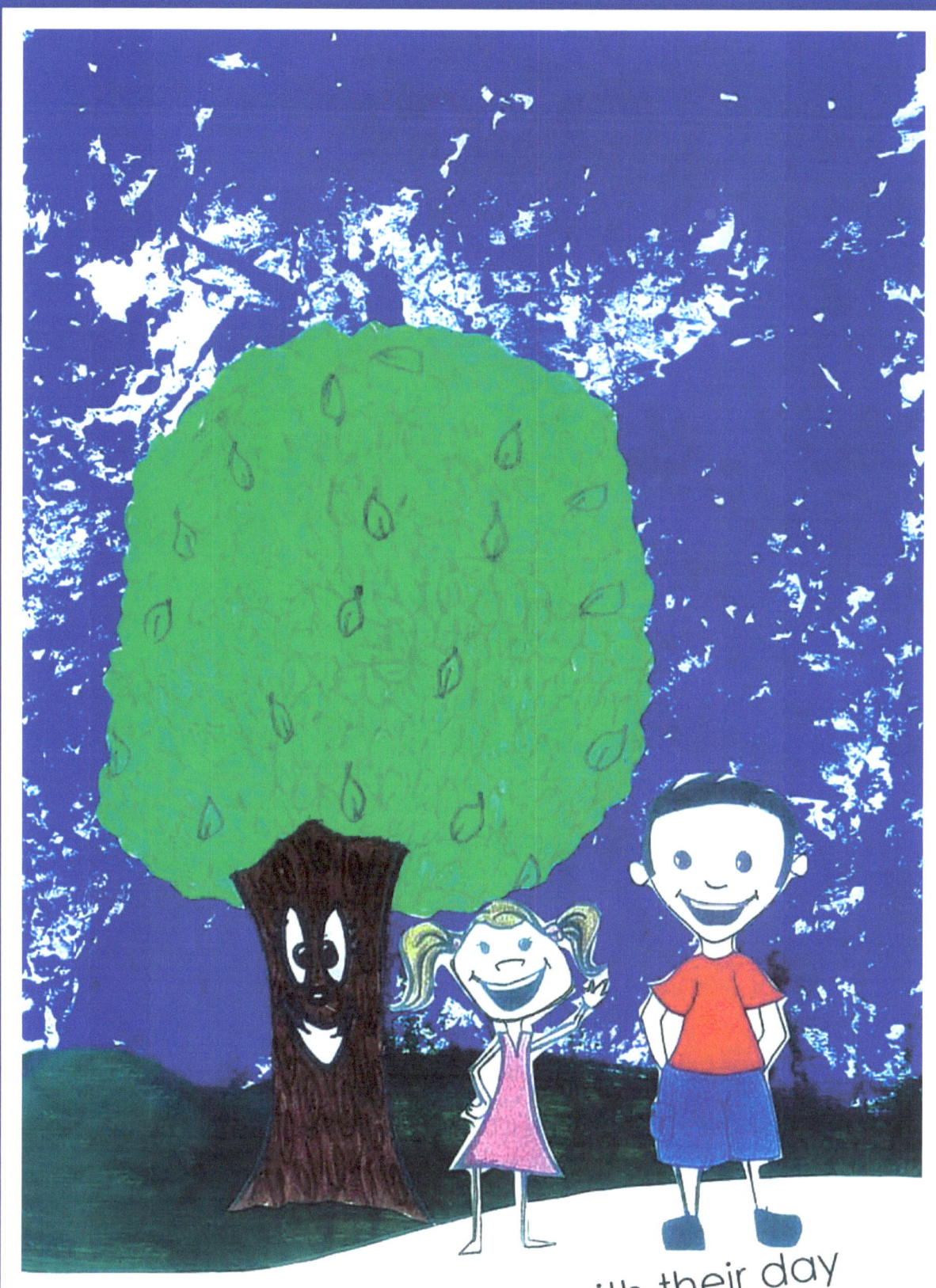

When they are finished with their day

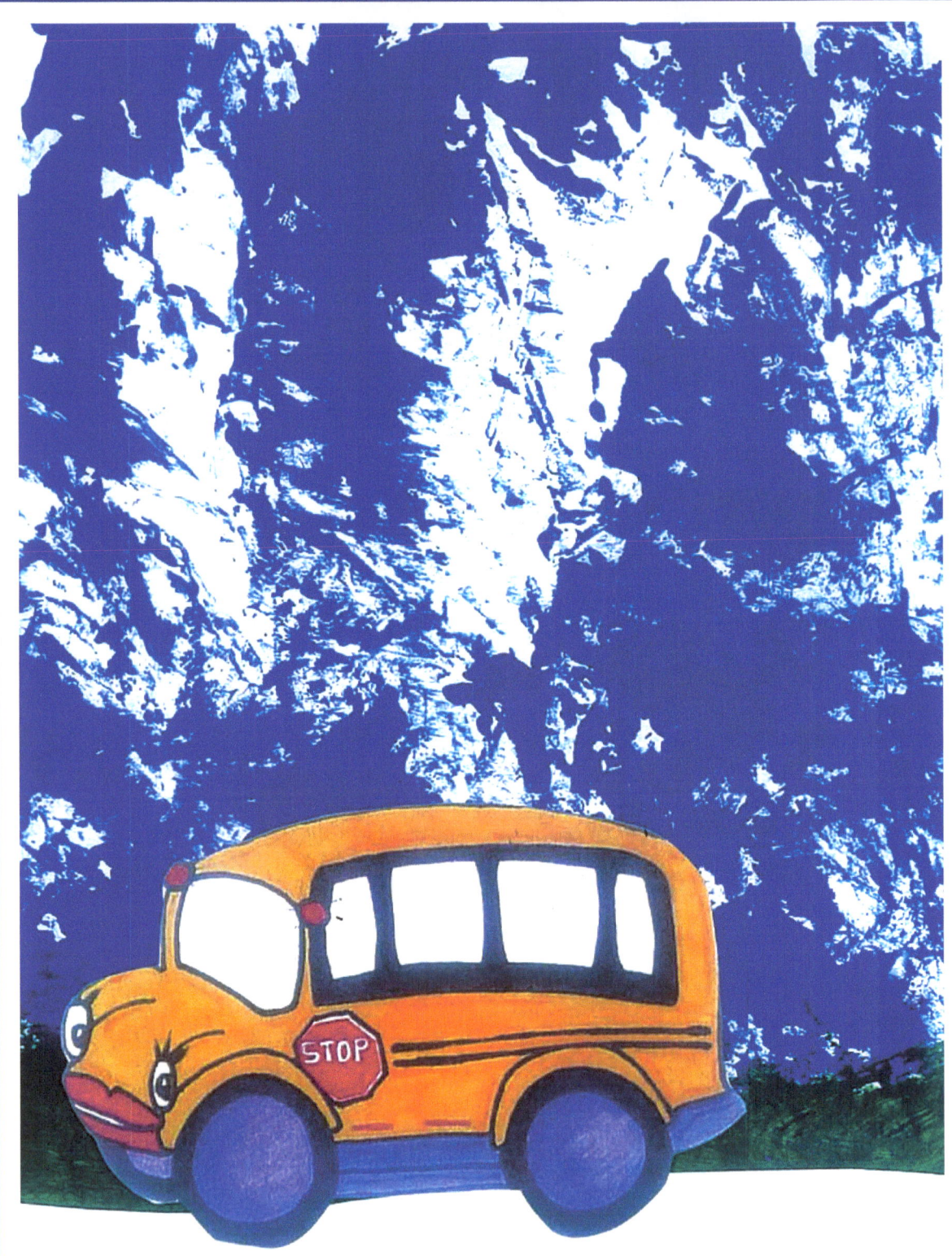

Sammy will take them on their way.

Some things to review.

What characters are in the book?

What colors are on the traffic light?

What does red say?

What does green say?

What does yellow say?

Find the words that rhyme.

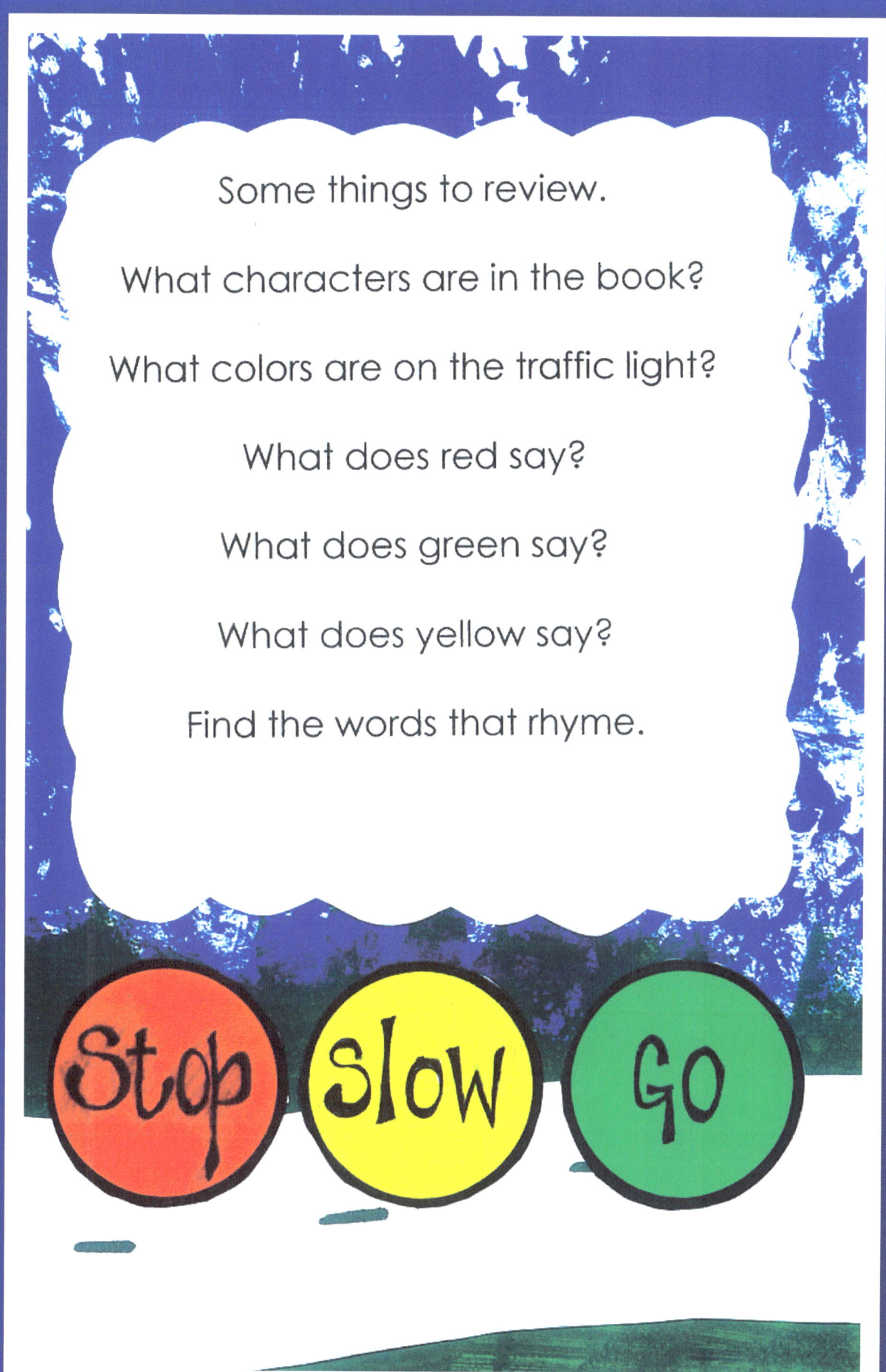

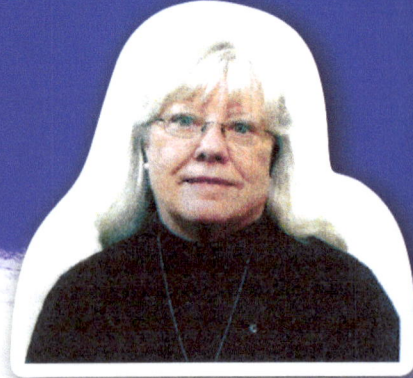

CAROL DUDLEY CO-AUTHOR

Lives in Tallahassee, florida, with her golden retreiver, Barney, and near her two sons and grandchildren.

CHERYL DANCE CO-AUTHOR

A retired preschool teacher, lives in Tallahassee, Florida, with her husband, Donnie, and near her two sons. Six grandchildren and one great-grandchild.

AMANDA COAR ILLUSTRATOR

Lives in Fort Myers, Florida with her fiance', Justin and step-daughter, Kailey.

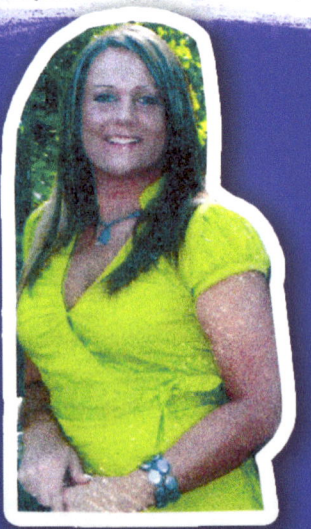